AF428121

SOLVING MULTI-STEP WORD PROBLEMS

Math Workbooks Grade 3
Children's Math Books

Solve the word problems!

Show your work.

1) Before getting to school, Sally has a few errands to run. Sally has to walk 12 blocks to the library, and 7 blocks to the store, before walking the final 11 blocks to arrive at school. If Sally has already walked 8 blocks, how many more blocks must she walk before arriving at school?

2) Sara wanted to save money to buy a new outfit. Sara saved $28.00 in April, $26.80 in May and $28.10 in June. However, she also had to spend $30.00 on school supplies and $43.00 on her dog. If the outfit costs $129.50, how much money does Sara still need to save?

3) Joan had 166 wolf stickers. Joan gave 40 stickers to John, 46 stickers to her sister and an additional 52 stickers to Benny. How many stickers does Joan still have?

1) Sally wants several different color plates for her birthday. Sally wants to get 84 yellow plates, 72 cyan plates, and some amount of green plates. In total, Sally wants 252 plates, so how many green plates should she get?

2) At an amusement park, Nancy wants to ride a rollercoaster that costs 35 tickets, a bumper car that costs 20 tickets, and a merry-go-round that costs 29 tickets. Nancy had 16 tickets, but lost 6 of them on a ride. How many more tickets does she need?

3) Nancy made 3 different stacks of wooden blocks. The first stack was 7 blocks high, the second stack was 6 block(s) higher than the first, and the final stack was 7 block(s) higher than the second. In total, how many blocks did Nancy use for all 3 stacks?

EXERCISE NO. 3

1) Keith wants several different color plates for his birthday. Keith wants to get 108 black plates, 144 cyan plates, and some amount of yellow plates. In total, Keith wants 384 plates, so how many yellow plates should he get?

2) Fred made 3 different stacks of wooden blocks. The first stack was 4 blocks high, the second stack was 11 block(s) higher than the first, and the final stack was 4 block(s) higher than the second. In total, how many blocks did Fred use for all 3 stacks?

3) Sally wanted to save money to buy a new outfit. Sally saved $25.70 in March, $26.50 in April and $20.00 in May. However, she also had to spend $21.20 on school supplies and $42.00 on her dog. If the outfit costs $185.60, how much money does Sally still need to save?

EXERCISE NO. 4

1) For lunch, John bought a glass of juice for $1.60, a tuna sandwich for $4.10, as well as some sherbet for $3.00. The tax came out to $1.50, and John paid with $17.00. How much change should John receive?

2) Joan had 164 deer stickers. Joan gave 32 stickers to John, 29 stickers to her sister and an additional 36 stickers to Fred. How many stickers does Joan still have?

3) For bowling season, Mike decided to buy a ball for $6.20, new shorts for $20.50, as well as a pair of bowling shoes for $44.40. Mike currently has $15.50, and a coupon for $13.00 off his purchase. How much more money does Mike need to complete his purchase?

EXERCISE NO. 5

1) Keith likes to collect coins. Keith got 19 coins from his brother, 25 coins from his mother, as well as 36 coins from Sara. However, Keith lost 24 coins before putting those coins into his piggybank. How many coins does Keith have in his piggybank?

2) For lacrosse season, Jess decided to buy a ball for $7.50, new shorts for $19.30, as well as a pair of lacrosse shoes for $40.90. Jess currently has $25.90, and a coupon for $11.00 off her purchase. How much more money does Jess need to complete her purchase?

3) Before getting to school, Sally has a few errands to run. Sally has to walk 7 blocks to the library, and 8 blocks to the gallery, before walking the final 4 blocks to arrive at school. If Sally has already walked 11 blocks, how many more blocks must she walk before arriving at school?

1) Mike likes to collect coins. Mike got 33 coins from his brother, 30 coins from his mother, as well as 37 coins from Keith. However, Mike lost 19 coins before putting those coins into his piggybank. How many coins does Mike have in his piggybank?

2) Nancy wants several different color plates for her birthday. Nancy wants to get 84 green plates, 120 silver plates, and some amount of cyan plates. In total, Nancy wants 336 plates, so how many cyan plates should she get?

3) At an amusement park, Joan wants to ride a rollercoaster that costs 14 tickets, a bumper car that costs 30 tickets, and a merry-go-round that costs 25 tickets. Joan had 26 tickets, but lost 9 of them on a ride. How many more tickets does she need?

1) Mike wants 168 cupcakes for his party. Mike has already made 36 cocoa cupcakes, and 60 berry cupcakes. How many more cupcakes does Mike need to make?

2) At an amusement park, Mike wants to ride a rollercoaster that costs 14 tickets, a bumper car that costs 31 tickets, and a merry-go-round that costs 35 tickets. Mike had 25 tickets, but lost 7 of them on a ride. How many more tickets does he need?

3) For lacrosse season, Sandy decided to buy a ball for $7.60, new shorts for $25.80, as well as a pair of lacrosse shoes for $41.90. Sandy currently has $16.00, and a coupon for $10.00 off her purchase. How much more money does Sandy need to complete her purchase?

1) Jason made 3 different stacks of wooden blocks. The first stack was 7 blocks high, the second stack was 6 block(s) higher than the first, and the final stack was 7 block(s) higher than the second. In total, how many blocks did Jason use for all 3 stacks?

2) For football season, Sally decided to buy a ball for $9.80, new shorts for $15.30, as well as a pair of football shoes for $40.70. Sally currently has $29.60, and a coupon for $11.00 off her purchase. How much more money does Sally need to complete her purchase?

3) Mike wanted to save money to buy a new outfit. Mike saved $21.40 in June, $23.10 in July and $20.40 in August. However, he also had to spend $23.20 on school supplies and $47.20 on his dog. If the outfit costs $162.00, how much money does Mike still need to save?

EXERCISE NO. 9

1) Before getting to school, Benny has a few errands to run. Benny has to walk 6 blocks to the museum and 11 blocks to the store, before walking the final 8 blocks to arrive at school. If Benny has already walked 5 blocks, how many more blocks must he walk before arriving at school?

2) Peter made 3 different stacks of wooden blocks. The first stack was 4 blocks high, the second stack was 10 block(s) higher than the first, and the final stack was 4 block(s) higher than the second. In total, how many blocks did Peter use for all 3 stacks?

3) Mary wants several different color plates for her birthday. Mary wants to get 72 orange plates, 108 gold plates, and some amount of cyan plates. In total, Mary wants 300 plates, so how many cyan plates should she get?

EXERCISE NO. 10

1) Mike made 3 different stacks of wooden blocks. The first stack was 7 blocks high, the second stack was 3 block(s) higher than the first, and the final stack was 7 block(s) higher than the second. In total, how many blocks did Mike use for all 3 stacks?

2) Sally likes to collect coins. Sally got 37 coins from her brother, 16 coins from her mother, as well as 38 coins from Sandy. However, Sally lost 28 coins before putting those coins into her piggybank. How many coins does Sally have in her piggybank?

3) Sara had 258 deer stickers. Sara gave 50 stickers to Sandy, 77 stickers to her sister and an additional 68 stickers to Benny. How many stickers does Sara still have?

1) Jason wants several different color plates for his birthday. Jason wants to get 72 gold plates, 120 orange plates, and some amount of cyan plates. In total, Jason wants 300 plates, so how many cyan plates should he get?

2) Mary wants 156 cupcakes for her party. Mary has already made 72 cocoa cupcakes, and 24 vanilla cupcakes. How many more cupcakes does Mary need to make?

3) For lunch, Fred bought a glass of soda for $1.00, a venison sandwich for $5.30, as well as some cobbler for $2.70. The tax came out to $1.60, and Fred paid with $20.00. How much change should Fred receive?

EXERCISE NO. 12

1) Keith made 3 different stacks of wooden blocks. The first stack was 5 blocks high, the second stack was 5 block(s) higher than the first, and the final stack was 5 block(s) higher than the second. In total, how many blocks did Keith use for all 3 stacks?

2) For lunch, Fred bought a glass of soda for $1.70, a turkey sandwich for $4.60, as well as some cupcakes for $3.40. The tax came out to $1.00, and Fred paid with $15.00. How much change should Fred receive?

3) For lacrosse season, Sara decided to buy a ball for $8.50, new shorts for $25.90, as well as a pair of lacrosse shoes for $40.80. Sara currently has $29.20, and a coupon for $15.00 off her purchase. How much more money does Sara need to complete her purchase?

1) Before getting to school, Sally has a few errands to run. Sally has to walk 6 blocks to the gallery, and 10 blocks to the library, before walking the final 4 blocks to arrive at school. If Sally has already walked 8 blocks, how many more blocks must she walk before arriving at school?

2) For lunch, Mary bought a glass of soda for $1.60, a venison sandwich for $4.40, as well as some cupcakes for $2.70. The tax came out to $1.80, and Mary paid with $20.00. How much change should Mary receive?

3) Sandy wants 168 cupcakes for her party. Sandy has already made 72 cocoa cupcakes, and 60 cherry cupcakes. How many more cupcakes does Sandy need to make?

EXERCISE NO. 14

1) Mary wants several different color plates for her birthday. Mary wants to get 72 green plates, 144 gold plates, and some amount of yellow plates. In total, Mary wants 300 plates, so how many yellow plates should she get?

2) Sandy wanted to save money to buy a new outfit. Sandy saved $25.10 in May, $29.90 in June and $28.00 in July. However, she also had to spend $30.00 on school supplies and $41.60 on her dog. If the outfit costs $153.10, how much money does Sandy still need to save?

3) Fred likes to collect coins. Fred got 37 coins from his brother, 26 coins from his mother, as well as 29 coins from Sandy. However, Fred lost 21 coins before putting those coins into his piggybank. How many coins does Fred have in his piggybank?

EXERCISE NO. 15

1) At an amusement park, Joan wants to ride a rollercoaster that costs 19 tickets, a bumper car that costs 27 tickets, and a merry-go-round that costs 21 tickets. Joan had 22 tickets, but lost 7 of them on a ride. How many more tickets does she need?

2) Before getting to school, Sara has a few errands to run. Sara has to walk 9 blocks to the theater, and 11 blocks to the museum, before walking the final 6 blocks to arrive at school. If Sara has already walked 10 blocks, how many more blocks must she walk before arriving at school?

3) Sally likes to collect coins. Sally got 33 coins from her brother, 22 coins from her mother, as well as 27 coins from Joan. However, Sally lost 25 coins before putting those coins into her piggybank. How many coins does Sally have in her piggybank?

EXERCISE NO. 16

1) Peter wanted to save money to buy a new outfit. Peter saved $23.30 in April, $21.80 in May and $24.40 in June. However, he also had to spend $26.50 on school supplies and $40.50 on his dog. If the outfit costs $151.50, how much money does Peter still need to save?

2) Fred had 210 wolf stickers. Fred gave 40 stickers to Sandy, 44 stickers to his sister and an additional 59 stickers to Sally. How many stickers does Fred still have?

3) For lunch, Jess bought a glass of juice for $1.00, a venison sandwich for $4.70, as well as some cookies for $3.20. The tax came out to $1.80, and Jess paid with $15.00. How much change should Jess receive?

EXERCISE NO. 17

1) Mary likes to collect coins. Mary got 34 coins from her brother, 38 coins from her mother, as well as 25 coins from Sandy. However, Mary lost 35 coins before putting those coins into her piggybank. How many coins does Mary have in her piggybank?

2) For baseball season, Benny decided to buy a ball for $6.90, new shorts for $25.00, as well as a pair of baseball shoes for $42.20. Benny currently has $20.70, and a coupon for $14.00 off his purchase. How much more money does Benny need to complete his purchase?

3) For lunch, Nancy bought a glass of milk for $1.00, a bacon sandwich for $4.10, as well as some cobbler for $2.50. The tax came out to $1.60, and Nancy paid with $17.00. How much change should Nancy receive?

EXERCISE NO. 18

1) For bowling season, Sally decided to buy a ball for $6.00, new shorts for $19.10, as well as a pair of bowling shoes for $48.80. Sally currently has $24.30, and a coupon for $10.00 off her purchase. How much more money does Sally need to complete her purchase?

2) At an amusement park, Peter wants to ride a rollercoaster that costs 14 tickets, a bumper car that costs 19 tickets, and a merry-go-round that costs 31 tickets. Peter had 22 tickets, but lost 6 of them on a ride. How many more tickets does he need?

3) For lunch, Mary bought a glass of juice for $1.80, a chicken sandwich for $4.20, as well as some sherbet for $2.10. The tax came out to $1.50, and Mary paid with $17.00. How much change should Mary receive?

1) Before getting to school, Sara has a few errands to run. Sara has to walk 9 blocks to the museum, and 8 blocks to the gallery, before walking the final 11 blocks to arrive at school. If Sara has already walked 10 blocks, how many more blocks must she walk before arriving at school?

2) Sally likes to collect coins. Sally got 34 coins from her brother, 21 coins from her mother, as well as 37 coins from Sandy. However, Sally lost 38 coins before putting those coins into her piggybank. How many coins does Sally have in her piggybank?

3) Sara wanted to save money to buy a new outfit. Sara saved $29.40 in June, $22.60 in July and $26.90 in August. However, she also had to spend $22.60 on school supplies and $49.00 on her dog. If the outfit costs $133.40, how much money does Sara still need to save?

EXERCISE NO. 20

1) At an amusement park, Benny wants to ride a rollercoaster that costs 22 tickets, a bumper car that costs 28 tickets, and a merry-go-round that costs 31 tickets. Benny had 29 tickets, but lost 9 of them on a ride. How many more tickets does he need?

2) John wanted to save money to buy a new outfit. John saved $22.60 in April, $24.30 in May and $27.20 in June. However, he also had to spend $21.40 on school supplies and $40.60 on his dog. If the outfit costs $145.00, how much money does John still need to save?

3) Joan made 3 different stacks of wooden blocks. The first stack was 4 blocks high, the second stack was 10 block(s) higher than the first, and the final stack was 4 block(s) higher than the second. In total, how many blocks did Joan use for all 3 stacks?

1) Jess had 205 bear stickers. Jess gave 67 stickers to Joan, 80 stickers to her sister and an additional 38 stickers to Fred. How many stickers does Jess still have?

2) Fred wants 144 cupcakes for his party. Fred has already made 48 cocoa cupcakes, and 36 mocha cupcakes. How many more cupcakes does Fred need to make?

3) Sandy wanted to save money to buy a new outfit. Sandy saved $27.60 in May, $29.80 in June and $26.90 in July. However, she also had to spend $19.80 on school supplies and $48.30 on her dog. If the outfit costs $172.30, how much money does Sandy still need to save?

EXERCISE NO. 22

1) Benny wants 180 cupcakes for his party. Benny has already made 60 vanilla cupcakes, and 48 fudge cupcakes. How many more cupcakes does Benny need to make?

2) At an amusement park, Sara wants to ride a rollercoaster that costs 15 tickets, a bumper car that costs 14 tickets, and a merry-go-round that costs 32 tickets. Sara had 29 tickets, but lost 8 of them on a ride. How many more tickets does she need?

3) John wanted to save money to buy a new outfit. John saved $29.00 in June, $20.90 in July and $25.90 in August. However, he also had to spend $27.00 on school supplies and $45.00 on his dog. If the outfit costs $166.60, how much money does John still need to save?

1) Before getting to school, Sandy has a few errands to run. Sandy has to walk 11 blocks to the theater, and 9 blocks to the store, before walking the final 4 blocks to arrive at school. If Sandy has already walked 7 blocks, how many more blocks must she walk before arriving at school?

2) Sandy had 177 wolf stickers. Sandy gave 31 stickers to John, 68 stickers to her sister and an additional 51 stickers to Mary. How many stickers does Sandy still have?

3) For lunch, John bought a glass of milk for $1.00, a tuna sandwich for $4.50, as well as some sherbet for $2.80. The tax came out to $1.70, and John paid with $18.00. How much change should John receive?

EXERCISE NO. 24

1) Keith had 225 lynx stickers. Keith gave 24 stickers to Benny, 74 stickers to his sister and an additional 75 stickers to Sandy. How many stickers does Keith still have?

2) For lunch, Mary bought a glass of milk for $1.50, a turkey sandwich for $5.50, as well as some cupcakes for $2.70. The tax came out to $1.80, and Mary paid with $20.00. How much change should Mary receive?

3) Jason wanted to save money to buy a new outfit. Jason saved $26.60 in April, $28.20 in May and $28.60 in June. However, he also had to spend $15.90 on school supplies and $49.50 on his dog. If the outfit costs $109.50, how much money does Jason still need to save?

EXERCISE NO. 25

1) At an amusement park, Benny wants to ride a rollercoaster that costs 30 tickets, a bumper car that costs 18 tickets, and a merry-go-round that costs 15 tickets. Benny had 23 tickets, but lost 7 of them on a ride. How many more tickets does he need?

2) Before getting to school, Jason has a few errands to run. Jason has to walk 11 blocks to the library, and 7 blocks to the museum, before walking the final 5 blocks to arrive at school. If Jason has already walked 9 blocks, how many more blocks must he walk before arriving at school?

3) For football season, John decided to buy a ball for $5.30, new shorts for $16.60, as well as a pair of football shoes for $44.30. John currently has $15.90, and a coupon for $13.00 off his purchase. How much more money does John need to complete his purchase?

EXERCISE NO. 26

1) For lunch, Nancy bought a glass of water for $1.80, a chicken sandwich for $5.30, as well as some cupcakes for $2.00. The tax came out to $1.00, and Nancy paid with $16.00. How much change should Nancy receive?

2) Sandy made 3 different stacks of wooden blocks. The first stack was 5 blocks high, the second stack was 7 block(s) higher than the first, and the final stack was 5 block(s) higher than the second. In total, how many blocks did Sandy use for all 3 stacks?

3) Jess wanted to save money to buy a new outfit. Jess saved $28.50 in April, $22.20 in May and $29.80 in June. However, she also had to spend $18.30 on school supplies and $48.40 on her dog. If the outfit costs $116.50, how much money does Jess still need to save?

EXERCISE NO. 27

1) For football season, Jason decided to buy a ball for $6.60, new shorts for $27.80, as well as a pair of football shoes for $41.80. Jason currently has $25.20, and a coupon for $13.00 off his purchase. How much more money does Jason need to complete his purchase?

2) Mike had 250 tiger stickers. Mike gave 77 stickers to Sally, 76 stickers to his sister and an additional 74 stickers to Jason. How many stickers does Mike still have?

3) Before getting to school, Peter has a few errands to run. Peter has to walk 12 blocks to the store, and 11 blocks to the library, before walking the final 6 blocks to arrive at school. If Peter has already walked 10 blocks, how many more blocks must he walk before arriving at school?

EXERCISE NO. 28

1) Jason likes to collect coins. Jason got 16 coins from his brother, 21 coins from his mother, as well as 35 coins from Sally. However, Jason lost 20 coins before putting those coins into his piggybank. How many coins does Jason have in his piggybank?

2) Keith wants 144 cupcakes for his party. Keith has already made 48 cherry cupcakes, and 36 cocoa cupcakes. How many more cupcakes does Keith need to make?

3) For lacrosse season, Sandy decided to buy a ball for $7.60, new shorts for $25.20, as well as a pair of lacrosse shoes for $47.70. Sandy currently has $20.00, and a coupon for $10.00 off her purchase. How much more money does Sandy need to complete her purchase?

EXERCISE NO. 29

1) For lacrosse season, Fred decided to buy a ball for $6.20, new shorts for $29.80, as well as a pair of lacrosse shoes for $48.70. Fred currently has $26.20, and a coupon for $14.00 off his purchase. How much more money does Fred need to complete his purchase?

2) Mike wants several different color plates for his birthday. Mike wants to get 132 green plates, 72 orange plates, and some amount of gold plates. In total, Mike wants 324 plates, so how many gold plates should he get?

3) Sandy likes to collect coins. Sandy got 36 coins from her brother, 26 coins from her mother, as well as 34 coins from Jason. However, Sandy lost 28 coins before putting those coins into her piggybank. How many coins does Sandy have in her piggybank?

EXERCISE NO. 30

1) Peter wants 120 cupcakes for his party. Peter has already made 24 cherry cupcakes, and 60 berry cupcakes. How many more cupcakes does Peter need to make?

2) Mike made 3 different stacks of wooden blocks. The first stack was 8 blocks high, the second stack was 2 block(s) higher than the first, and the final stack was 8 block(s) higher than the second. In total, how many blocks did Mike use for all 3 stacks?

3) John had 220 kitty stickers. John gave 62 stickers to Sally, 67 stickers to his sister and an additional 64 stickers to Mary. How many stickers does John still have?

1) Jason made 3 different stacks of wooden blocks. The first stack was 8 blocks high, the second stack was 3 block(s) higher than the first, and the final stack was 8 block(s) higher than the second. In total, how many blocks did Jason use for all 3 stacks?

2) Jason wants 132 cupcakes for his party. Jason has already made 24 fudge cupcakes, and 48 cherry cupcakes. How many more cupcakes does Jason need to make?

3) Mike wanted to save money to buy a new outfit. Mike saved $28.70 in June, $21.80 in July and $28.90 in August. However, he also had to spend $19.60 on school supplies and $45.80 on his dog. If the outfit costs $107.90, how much money does Mike still need to save?

EXERCISE NO. 32

1) Before getting to school, Peter has a few errands to run. Peter has to walk 5 blocks to the museum, and 7 blocks to the gallery, before walking the final 6 blocks to arrive at school. If Peter has already walked 9 blocks, how many more blocks must he walk before arriving at school?

2) Mike had 196 lion stickers. Mike gave 35 stickers to Joan, 54 stickers to his sister and an additional 73 stickers to Keith. How many stickers does Mike still have?

3) At an amusement park, Sara wants to ride a rollercoaster that costs 26 tickets, a bumper car that costs 35 tickets, and a merry-go-round that costs 23 tickets. Sara had 29 tickets, but lost 9 of them on a ride. How many more tickets does she need?

EXERCISE NO. 33

1) Before getting to school, Peter has a few errands to run. Peter has to walk 6 blocks to the library, and 11 blocks to the store, before walking the final 5 blocks to arrive at school. If Peter has already walked 10 blocks, how many more blocks must he walk before arriving at school?

2) For soccer season, Sara decided to buy a ball for $7.30, new shorts for $25.10, as well as a pair of soccer shoes for $47.70. Sara currently has $25.30, and a coupon for $15.00 off her purchase. How much more money does Sara need to complete her purchase?

3) Sally wants 144 cupcakes for her party. Sally has already made 72 mocha cupcakes, and 24 berry cupcakes. How many more cupcakes does Sally need to make?

1) Mike had 165 deer stickers. Mike gave 42 stickers to Peter, 28 stickers to his sister and an additional 49 stickers to Nancy. How many stickers does Mike still have?

2) Nancy likes to collect coins. Nancy got 26 coins from her brother, 21 coins from her mother, as well as 23 coins from Sally. However, Nancy lost 17 coins before putting those coins into her piggybank. How many coins does Nancy have in her piggybank?

3) For bowling season, Nancy decided to buy a ball for $7.70, new shorts for $18.40, as well as a pair of bowling shoes for $44.40. Nancy currently has $21.40, and a coupon for $10.00 off her purchase. How much more money does Nancy need to complete her purchase?

EXERCISE NO. 35

1) Fred had 250 wolf stickers. Fred gave 57 stickers to Jess, 65 stickers to his sister and an additional 59 stickers to John. How many stickers does Fred still have?

2) Benny wanted to save money to buy a new outfit. Benny saved $29.00 in March, $23.50 in April and $27.60 in May. However, he also had to spend $23.80 on school supplies and $42.00 on his dog. If the outfit costs $144.20, how much money does Benny still need to save?

3) Before getting to school, Mary has a few errands to run. Mary has to walk 10 blocks to the museum, and 7 blocks to the store, before walking the final 11 blocks to arrive at school. If Mary has already walked 6 blocks, how many more blocks must she walk before arriving at school?

EXERCISE NO. 36

1) Sally likes to collect coins. Sally got 38 coins from her brother, 26 coins from her mother, as well as 35 coins from Keith. However, Sally lost 37 coins before putting those coins into her piggybank. How many coins does Sally have in her piggybank?

2) Mike had 208 kitty stickers. Mike gave 75 stickers to Nancy, 26 stickers to his sister and an additional 80 stickers to Mary. How many stickers does Mike still have?

3) Peter wants 108 cupcakes for his party. Peter has already made 48 mocha cupcakes, and 36 cherry cupcakes. How many more cupcakes does Peter need to make?

EXERCISE NO. 37

1) John wanted to save money to buy a new outfit. John saved $26.50 in April, $25.30 in May and $20.40 in June. However, he also had to spend $26.90 on school supplies and $48.60 on his dog. If the outfit costs $141.40, how much money does John still need to save?

2) Benny wants 144 cupcakes for his party. Benny has already made 72 mocha cupcakes, and 48 fudge cupcakes. How many more cupcakes does Benny need to make?

3) For softball season, Nancy decided to buy a ball for $8.90, new shorts for $21.00, as well as a pair of softball shoes for $46.40. Nancy currently has $20.90, and a coupon for $12.00 off her purchase. How much more money does Nancy need to complete her purchase?

1) Mike wanted to save money to buy a new outfit. Mike saved $21.40 in April, $23.80 in May and $21.60 in June. However, he also had to spend $23.70 on school supplies and $41.80 on his dog. If the outfit costs $199.10, how much money does Mike still need to save?

2) Mary likes to collect coins. Mary got 17 coins from her brother, 23 coins from her mother, as well as 33 coins from Jess. However, Mary lost 35 coins before putting those coins into her piggybank. How many coins does Mary have in her piggybank?

3) John wants 144 cupcakes for his party. John has already made 72 fudge cupcakes, and 48 cherry cupcakes. How many more cupcakes does John need to make?

EXERCISE NO. 39

1) Before getting to school, Joan has a few errands to run. Joan has to walk 5 blocks to the museum, and 12 blocks to the gallery, before walking the final 8 blocks to arrive at school. If Joan has already walked 11 blocks, how many more blocks must she walk before arriving at school?

2) For baseball season, Fred decided to buy a ball for $8.50, new shorts for $28.60, as well as a pair of baseball shoes for $46.50. Fred currently has $26.90, and a coupon for $10.00 off his purchase. How much more money does Fred need to complete his purchase?

3) Keith likes to collect coins. Keith got 29 coins from his brother, 18 coins from his mother, as well as 32 coins from Mike. However, Keith lost 31 coins before putting those coins into his piggybank. How many coins does Keith have in his piggybank?

1) Sandy wanted to save money to buy a new outfit. Sandy saved $26.40 in May, $24.50 in June and $20.60 in July. However, she also had to spend $21.70 on school supplies and $41.80 on her dog. If the outfit costs $195.60, how much money does Sandy still need to save?

2) Mary had 173 tiger stickers. Mary gave 35 stickers to Jess, 30 stickers to her sister and an additional 66 stickers to Jason. How many stickers does Mary still have?

3) Keith made 3 different stacks of wooden blocks. The first stack was 5 blocks high, the second stack was 8 block(s) higher than the first, and the final stack was 5 block(s) higher than the second. In total, how many blocks did Keith use for all 3 stacks?

EXERCISE NO. 41

1) Fred likes to collect coins. Fred got 27 coins from his brother, 28 coins from his mother, as well as 34 coins from Sara. However, Fred lost 24 coins before putting those coins into his piggybank. How many coins does Fred have in his piggybank?

2) At an amusement park, Jason wants to ride a rollercoaster that costs 22 tickets, a bumper car that costs 25 tickets, and a merry-go-round that costs 27 tickets. Jason had 31 tickets, but lost 9 of them on a ride. How many more tickets does he need?

3) Benny wanted to save money to buy a new outfit. Benny saved $29.00 in March, $24.50 in April and $27.60 in May. However, he also had to spend $20.50 on school supplies and $49.00 on his dog. If the outfit costs $108.60, how much money does Benny still need to save?

EXERCISE NO. 42

1) For lunch, John bought a glass of juice for $1.80, a turkey sandwich for $4.80, as well as some cupcakes for $2.70. The tax came out to $1.10, and John paid with $15.00. How much change should John receive?

2) Peter wants several different color plates for his birthday. Peter wants to get 72 cyan plates, 132 green plates, and some amount of silver plates. In total, Peter wants 300 plates, so how many silver plates should he get?

3) Nancy likes to collect coins. Nancy got 34 coins from her brother, 33 coins from her mother, as well as 20 coins from Jason. However, Nancy lost 24 coins before putting those coins into her piggybank. How many coins does Nancy have in her piggybank?

1) Peter wants several different color plates for his birthday. Peter wants to get 144 orange plates, 120 silver plates, and some amount of gold plates. In total, Peter wants 336 plates, so how many gold plates should he get?

2) Benny wanted to save money to buy a new outfit. Benny saved $20.40 in March, $27.60 in April and $26.90 in May. However, he also had to spend $28.50 on school supplies and $42.90 on his dog. If the outfit costs $154.20, how much money does Benny still need to save?

3) Nancy made 3 different stacks of wooden blocks. The first stack was 4 blocks high, the second stack was 7 block(s) higher than the first, and the final stack was 4 block(s) higher than the second. In total, how many blocks did Nancy use for all 3 stacks?

EXERCISE NO. 44

1) Jess wants several different color plates for her birthday. Jess wants to get 132 black plates, 72 yellow plates, and some amount of silver plates. In total, Jess wants 312 plates, so how many silver plates should she get?

2) Before getting to school, Sandy has a few errands to run. Sandy has to walk 8 blocks to the gallery, and 9 blocks to the library, before walking the final 11 blocks to arrive at school. If Sandy has already walked 6 blocks, how many more blocks must she walk before arriving at school?

3) Nancy likes to collect coins. Nancy got 27 coins from her brother, 25 coins from her mother, as well as 26 coins from Sandy. However, Nancy lost 24 coins before putting those coins into her piggybank. How many coins does Nancy have in her piggybank?

1) Benny wanted to save money to buy a new outfit. Benny saved $29.10 in May, $24.70 in June and $23.50 in July. However, he also had to spend $19.10 on school supplies and $47.80 on his dog. If the outfit costs $123.70, how much money does Benny still need to save?

2) Sara wants several different color plates for her birthday. Sara wants to get 96 green plates, 132 yellow plates, and some amount of black plates. In total, Sara wants 348 plates, so how many black plates should she get?

3) Before getting to school, Sandy has a few errands to run. Sandy has to walk 11 blocks to the museum and 5 blocks to the store, before walking the final 9 blocks to arrive at school. If Sandy has already walked 4 blocks, how many more blocks must she walk before arriving at school?

EXERCISE NO. 46

1) Sandy had 182 bear stickers. Sandy gave 46 stickers to Sally, 56 stickers to her sister and an additional 47 stickers to Peter. How many stickers does Sandy still have?

2) For bowling season, Benny decided to buy a ball for $9.20, new shorts for $22.40, as well as a pair of bowling shoes for $40.60. Benny currently has $29.80, and a coupon for $14.00 off his purchase. How much more money does Benny need to complete his purchase?

3) Mike wants several different color plates for his birthday. Mike wants to get 144 gold plates, 120 green plates, and some amount of yellow plates. In total, Mike wants 348 plates, so how many yellow plates should he get?

EXERCISE NO. 1

22 blocks

$119.60

28 stickers

EXERCISE NO. 2

96 plates

74 tickets

40 blocks

132 plates

38 blocks

$176.60

$6.80

67 stickers

$42.60

56 coins

$30.80

8 blocks

81 coins

132 plates

52 tickets

EXERCISE NO. 7

72 cupcakes

62 tickets

$49.30

EXERCISE NO. 8

40 blocks

$25.20

$167.50

EXERCISE NO. 9

20 blocks

36 blocks

120 plates

EXERCISE NO. 10

34 blocks

63 coins

63 stickers

108 plates

60 cupcakes

$9.40

30 blocks

$4.30

$31.00

12 blocks

$9.50

36 cupcakes

84 plates

$141.70

71 coins

EXERCISE NO. 15

52 tickets

16 blocks

57 coins

EXERCISE NO. 16

$149.00

67 stickers

$4.30

EXERCISE NO. 17

62 coins

$39.40

$7.80

EXERCISE NO. 18

$39.60

48 tickets

$7.40

18 blocks

54 coins

$126.10

61 tickets

$132.90

36 blocks

20 stickers

60 cupcakes

$156.10

72 cupcakes

40 tickets

$162.80

17 blocks
____

27 stickers
____

$8.00
____

52 stickers
____

$8.50
____

$91.50
____

47 tickets
____

14 blocks
____

$37.30
____

$5.90
____

34 blocks
____

$102.70
____

$38.00

23 stickers

19 blocks

52 coins

60 cupcakes

$50.50

$44.50

120 plates

68 coins

36 cupcakes

36 blocks

27 stickers

38 blocks

60 cupcakes

$93.90

9 blocks

34 stickers

64 tickets

12 blocks

$39.80

48 cupcakes

46 stickers

53 coins

$39.10

69 stickers

$129.90

22 blocks

62 coins

27 stickers

24 cupcakes

$144.70

24 cupcakes

$43.40

$197.80

38 coins

24 cupcakes

EXERCISE NO. 39

14 blocks
____

$46.70
____

48 coins
____

EXERCISE NO. 40

$187.60
____

42 stickers
____

36 blocks
____

EXERCISE NO. 41

65 coins
____

52 tickets
____

$97.00
____

EXERCISE NO. 42

$4.60
____

96 plates
____

63 coins
____

72 plates

____

$150.70

____

30 blocks

____

108 plates

____

22 blocks

____

54 coins

____

$113.30

____

120 plates

____

21 blocks

____

33 stickers

____

$28.40

____

84 plates

____

Visit

BABY PROFESSOR
EDUCATION KIDS

www.BabyProfessorBooks.com

to download Free Baby Professor eBooks
and view our catalog of new and exciting
Children's Books